Seeing

in Living Things

Karen Hartley, Chris Macro, and Philip Taylor

Heinemann Library
Chicago, Illinois

Designed by Celia Floyd
Illustrated by Alan Fraser
Originated by Ambassador Litho
Printed in Hong Kong / China

04 03 02 01 00
10 9 8 7 6 5 4 3 2 1

Library of Congress Cataloging-in-Publication Data
Hartley, Karen, 1949-
       Seeing in the living things / Karen Hartley, Chris Macro, and Philip
Taylor.
          p. cm. — (Senses.)
       Includes bibliographical references and index.
       Summary: Describes how the sense of sight works in humans and
animals and how they use it.
       ISBN 1-57572-247-X (lib. bdg.)
       1. Vision Juvenile literature. 2. Eye Juvenile literature.
[1. Vision. 2. Eye. 3. Senses and sensation.] I. Macro, Chris,
1940- . II. Taylor, Philip, 1949- . III. Title. IV. Series:
Hartley, Karen, 1949-   Senses.
QP475.7.H 2000
573.8'8—dc21   99-38258
                                                                      CIP

Acknowledgments

The Publishers would like to thank the following for permission to reproduce photographs:

Ardea London/Liz Bomford, p. 19; Bruce Coleman/Geoffe Dore, p. 17; Bruce Coleman/Michael Glover, p. 29; Corbis/Andrew Brown, p. 10; George Lepp, p. 11; Heinemann/Gareth Boden, pp. 4, 5, 6, 7, 8, 12, 13, 24, 25; Image Bank/Joseph Van Os, p. 16; Pictor International, pp. 18, 20; Sally Greenhill, p. 15; Tony Stone/Christopher Burki, p. 26; Tony Stone/Don Smetzer, p. 14; James Martin, p. 23; John Darling, p. 22; Renee Lynn, p. 21; Stephen Cooper, p. 28.

Cover photograph reproduced with permission of Oxford Scientific Films and Gareth Boden.

Every effort has been made to contact copyright holders of any material reproduced in this book. Any omissions will be rectified in subsequent printings if notice is given to the Publisher.

Some words are shown in bold, **like this**. You can find out what they mean by looking in the glossary.

CONTENTS

WHAT ARE YOUR SENSES?

Senses tell people and animals about the world around them. You use your senses to feel, see, hear, taste, and smell. Your senses make you feel good and warn you of danger.

Senses are important to you and other animals. This book is about the sense of sight. You will find out how sight works and what you use it for.

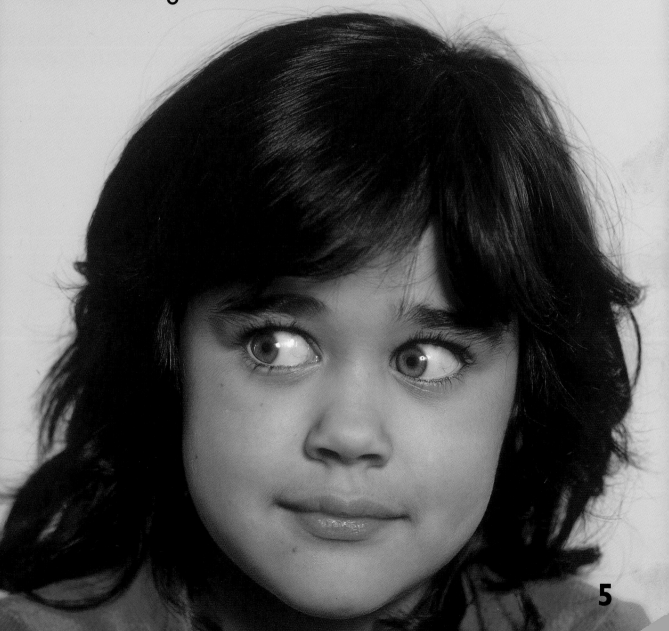

WHAT DO YOU USE TO SEE?

People use their eyes to see. You have two eyes at the front of your head. Animals use their eyes to see, too. Animals' eyes are not always at the front of their head.

You use both of your eyes together. This helps you see things that are near you and things that are far away. Your **eyelashes** and **eyelids** keep your eyes clean.

HOW DO YOU SEE?

Your eye is shaped like a ball. Most of the **eyeball** is inside your head. Eyeballs can move so that you can see things at the side and in front of you.

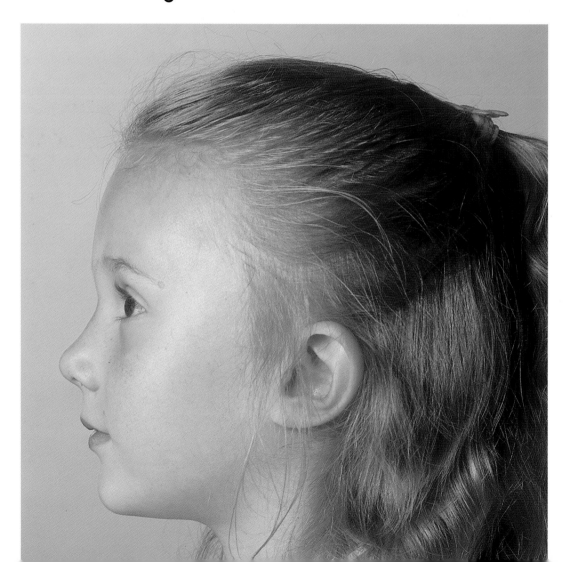

You need light to see. In the daytime you can see colors and shapes very well. At night you cannot see as well. Then things look gray or black.

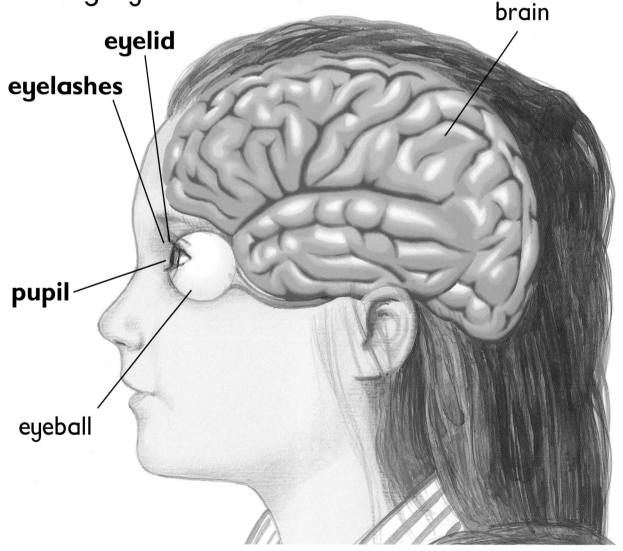

brain

eyelid

eyelashes

pupil

eyeball

KEEPING SAFE

You use your eyes to warn you of danger. You can see cars on the road and smoke from fires. You can read warning signs that help you stay away from danger.

People use their eyes to look for dangerous animals. You can also see if food is bad. Your eyes will tell you not eat it.

DO YOUR EYES HELP YOU?

You use your eyes to read stories and to watch television. You use your eyes to tell if a ball is close to you or far from you. You use your eyes when you work at a computer.

You need your eyes to use tools. Your eyes help you cut and measure. Adults use their eyes when they drive cars and trucks. Your eyes tell you when a friend is smiling.

WHAT CAN HAPPEN TO YOUR EYES?

Sometimes eyes do not work well. When this happens, people go to an **optician**. The optician makes glasses, so that people can see better.

Some people cannot see. They use their sense of touch and hearing to know where they are going. They use their fingers to read a special kind of writing called **braille**.

How Do Animals See?

Birds' eyes are not round like your eyes. Bird's eyes are shaped like an egg. This shape helps them see things that are far away.

Insects cannot move their eyes. They do not have **eyelids,** so their eyes are always open. Flies have hundreds of parts to their very big eyes. Flies can see all around them.

DO ANIMALS SEE LIKE YOU DO?

Some animals cannot see colors. Bulls, cats, owls, and bats cannot see colors. Cats and dogs have something like a mirror at the back of their eyes. This helps them see at night.

18

Moles live underground where it is dark. They cannot see well. They do not use their eyes much, but they can hear sounds well. Flies see hundreds of tiny pictures at one time.

HOW DO ANIMALS USE THEIR EYES?

Owls hunt at night. Their eyes are large to help them see in the dark. Their eyes look forward, so they can watch with both eyes at the same time.

Monkeys and apes have two eyes at the front of their head. This helps them to **focus.** They need to see tree branches clearly as they swing up and down.

HOW DO ANIMALS STAY SAFE?

Animals that hunt usually have two eyes at the front of their head. Animals that are eaten by other animals often have eyes at the sides of their head.

Rabbits have eyes at the sides of their head.
They can see almost all around them.
Chameleons can move each eye separately.
This helps them watch for danger.

INVESTIGATING SIGHT

Sit in a sunny place. Look into a mirror. The **pupil** in your eye is very small. Try this in a darker place. You will see that now the pupil is bigger. The **iris** around the pupil makes it bigger so more light can enter.

This girl is using a **periscope** to see what is over her head. The picture in the top mirror shines onto the bottom mirror. Then she can see what is above her.

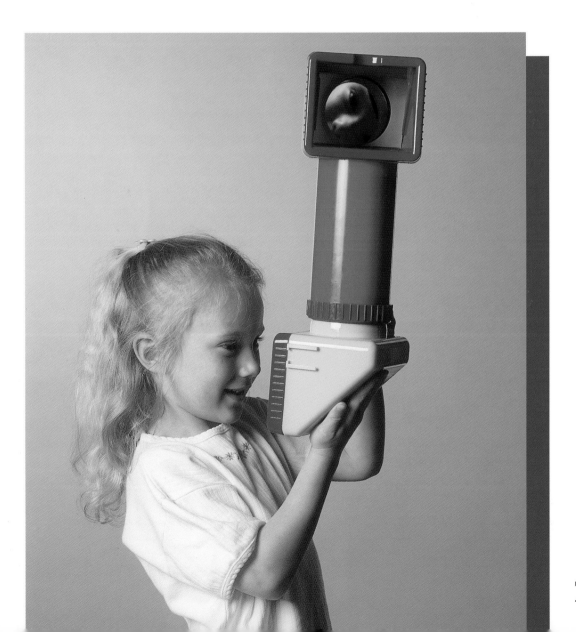

PLAYING TRICKS ON YOUR EYES

Animals that are the same color as things around them are difficult to see. We say they are **camouflaged**. Look at the picture. Do you see the camouflaged animal?

1. Trace a jar bottom onto paper.

2. Cut out the circles.

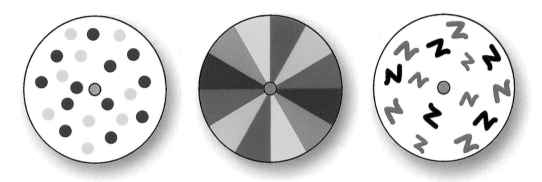

3. Draw colored patterns on the circles.

4. Push a pencil through the middle of each circle.

5. Quickly spin each circle. What do you see?

Are you surprised? When you spin the circles, different colors in the light bounce off the circles and into your eyes. Because the circles spin fast, the colors **blend**.

DID YOU KNOW?

Did you know that worms can tell the difference between light and dark? Did you know that snakes see through their **eyelids**?

Did you know that fish can see to the right and to the left at the same time?

Did you know that snails have eyes at the ends of their long **antennae**?

Did you know that honeybees can see colors, but they cannot see the color red?

GLOSSARY

antenna   (more than one are called antennae) long, thin growth on the head of an insect that helps the insect know what is around it

blend   mix together

braille   kind of writing with raised bumps on the paper that is read with the fingers

camouflaged   something that is the same color as the plants and land around it

chameleon   lizard that can change colors depending on light, hot, or cold

eyeball   ball-shaped part of the eye

eyelash   one of the hairs on the edge of the skin that covers your eye

eyelid   skin that covers the eyes when you blink or sleep

focus   to be able to see something clearly

iris   colored part around the pupil of the eye

lens   clear, oval part inside the eye that helps bend rays of light to make a clear picture of what is seen

optician   someone who makes and sells eyeglasses

optic nerve   part of the body that carries messages from the eye to the brain

periscope   long tube or box with mirrors at the top and bottom used to see things that are higher than people's heads

pupil   opening in the middle of the colored part of the eye

retina   back part of the eyeball that gets the light message

30

Sense Map

1. Light shines on the teddy bear.

2. The light goes in through the opening called the **pupil**.

3. The **lens** helps **focus** the light on the back of the eye.

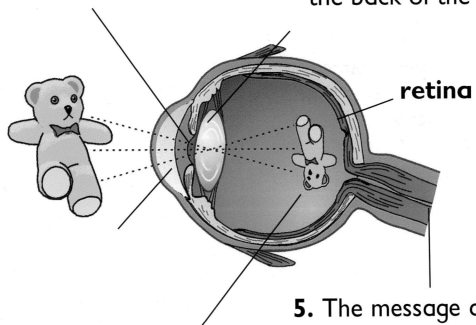

pupil

retina

4. The picture is turned upside down on the retina.

5. The message about the picture is sent to the brain by the **optic nerve.**

MORE BOOKS TO READ

Tatchell, Judy. *How Do Your Senses Work?* Tulsa, Okla.: E D C Publishing, 1998.

Hurwitz, Sue. *Sight.* New York: Rosen Publishing Group, 1997.

Pluckrose, Henry. *Seeing.* Milwaukee: Gareth Stevens, 1995.

INDEX